Francis Frith's
CAMBRIDGESHIRE

PHOTOGRAPHIC MEMORIES

Francis Frith's
CAMBRIDGESHIRE

◆

Clive Tully

FRITH
BOOK Co

First published in the United Kingdom in 2000 by
Frith Book Company Ltd

Hardback Edition 2000
ISBN 1-85937-086-1

Paperback Edition 2001
ISBN 1-85937-420-4

British Library Cataloguing in Publication Data

Francis Frith's Cambridgeshire
Clive Tully

Frith Book Company Ltd
Frith's Barn, Teffont,
Salisbury, Wiltshire SP3 5QP
Tel: +44 (0) 1722 716 376
Email: info@frithbook.co.uk
www.frithbook.co.uk

Printed and bound in Great Britain

CONTENTS

FRANCIS FRITH: *Victorian Pioneer*

FRANCIS FRITH, Victorian founder of the world-famous photographic archive, was a complex and multitudinous man. A devout Quaker and a highly successful Victorian businessman, he was both philosophic by nature and pioneering in outlook.

By 1855 Francis Frith had already established a wholesale grocery business in Liverpool, and sold it for the astonishing sum of £200,000, which is the equivalent today of over £15,000,000. Now a multi-millionaire, he was able to indulge his passion for travel. As a child he had pored over travel books written by early explorers, and his fancy and imagination had been stirred by family holidays to the sublime mountain regions of Wales and Scotland. 'What a land of spirit-stirring and enriching scenes and places!' he had written. He was to return to these scenes of grandeur in later years to 'recapture the thousands of vivid and tender memories', but with a different purpose. Now in his thirties, and captivated by the new science of photography, Frith set out on a series of pioneering journeys to the Nile regions that occupied him from 1856 until 1860.

INTRIGUE AND ADVENTURE

He took with him on his travels a specially-designed wicker carriage that acted as both dark-room and sleeping chamber. These far-flung journeys were packed with intrigue and adventure. In his life story, written when he was sixty-three, Frith tells of being held captive by bandits, and of fighting 'an awful midnight battle to the very point of surrender with a deadly pack of hungry, wild dogs'. Sporting flowing Arab costume, Frith arrived at Akaba by camel seventy years before Lawrence, where he encountered 'desert princes and rival sheikhs, blazing with jewel-hilted swords'.

During these extraordinary adventures he was assiduously exploring the desert regions bordering the Nile and patiently recording the antiquities and peoples with his camera. He was the first photographer to venture beyond the sixth cataract. Africa was still the mysterious 'Dark Continent', and Stanley and Livingstone's historic meeting was a decade into the future. The conditions for picture taking confound belief. He laboured for hours in his wicker dark-room in the sweltering heat of the desert, while the volatile chemicals fizzed dangerously in their trays. Often he was forced to work in remote tombs and caves where conditions were cooler. Back in London he exhibited his photographs and was 'rapturously cheered' by members of the Royal Society. His reputation as a photographer was made overnight. An eminent modern historian has likened their impact on the population of the time to that on our own generation of the first photographs taken on the surface of the moon.

VENTURE OF A LIFE-TIME

Characteristically, Frith quickly spotted the opportunity to create a new business as a specialist publisher of photographs. He lived in an era of immense and sometimes violent change. For the poor in the early part of Victoria's reign work was a drudge and the hours long, and people had precious little free time to enjoy themselves.

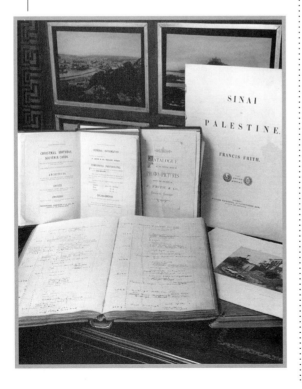

Most had no transport other than a cart or gig at their disposal, and had not travelled far beyond the boundaries of their own town or village. However, by the 1870s, the railways had threaded their way across the country, and Bank Holidays and half-day Saturdays had been made obligatory by Act of Parliament. All of a sudden the ordinary working man and his family were able to enjoy days out and see a little more of the world.

With characteristic business acumen, Francis Frith foresaw that these new tourists would enjoy having souvenirs to commemorate their days out. In 1860 he married Mary Ann Rosling and set out with the intention of photographing every city, town and village in Britain. For the next thirty years he travelled the country by train and by pony and trap, producing fine photographs of seaside resorts and beauty spots that were keenly bought by millions of Victorians. These prints were painstakingly pasted into family albums and pored over during the dark nights of winter, rekindling precious memories of summer excursions.

THE RISE OF FRITH & CO

Frith's studio was soon supplying retail shops all over the country. To meet the demand he gathered about him a small team of photographers, and published the work of independent artist-photographers of the calibre of Roger Fenton and Francis Bedford. In order to gain some understanding of the scale of Frith's business one only has to look at the catalogue issued by Frith & Co in 1886: it runs to some 670

pages, listing not only many thousands of views of the British Isles but also many photographs of most European countries, and China, Japan, the USA and Canada – note the sample page shown above from the hand-written *Frith & Co* ledgers detailing pictures taken. By 1890 Frith had created the greatest specialist photographic publishing company in the world, with over 2,000 outlets – more than the combined number that Boots and WH Smith have today! The picture on the right shows the *Frith & Co* display board at Ingleton in the Yorkshire Dales. Beautifully constructed with mahogany frame and gilt inserts, it could display up to a dozen local scenes.

POSTCARD BONANZA

The ever-popular holiday postcard we know today took many years to develop. In 1870 the Post Office issued the first plain cards, with a pre-printed stamp on one face. In 1894 they allowed other publishers' cards to be sent through the mail with an attached adhesive halfpenny stamp. Demand grew rapidly, and in 1895 a new size of postcard was permitted called the court card, but there was little room for illustration. In 1899, a year after Frith's death, a new card measuring 5.5 x 3.5 inches became the standard format, but it was not until 1902 that the divided back came into being, with address and message on one face and a full-size illustration on the other. *Frith & Co* were in the vanguard of postcard development, and Frith's sons Eustace and Cyril continued their father's monumental task, expanding the number of views offered to the public and recording more and more places in Britain, as the coasts and countryside were opened up to mass travel.

Francis Frith died in 1898 at his villa in Cannes, his great project still growing. The archive he created continued in business for another seventy years. By 1970 it contained over a third of a million pictures of 7,000 cities, towns and villages. The massive photographic record Frith has left to us stands as a living monument to a special and very remarkable man.

Frith's Archive: *A Unique Legacy*

FRANCIS FRITH'S legacy to us today is of immense significance and value, for the magnificent archive of evocative photographs he created provides a unique record of change in 7,000 cities, towns and villages throughout Britain over a century and more. Frith and his fellow studio photographers revisited locations many times down the years to update their views, compiling for us an enthralling and colourful pageant of British life and character.

We tend to think of Frith's sepia views of Britain as nostalgic, for most of us use them to conjure up memories of places in our own lives with which we have family associations. It often makes us forget that to Francis Frith they were records of daily life as it was actually being lived in the cities, towns and villages of his day. The Victorian age was one of great and often bewildering change for ordinary people, and though the pictures evoke an impression of slower times, life was as busy and hectic as it is today.

We are fortunate that Frith was a photographer of the people, dedicated to recording the minutiae of everyday life. For it is this sheer wealth of visual data, the painstaking chronicle of changes in dress, transport, street layouts, buildings, housing, engineering and landscape that captivates us so much today. His remarkable images offer us a powerful link with the past and with the lives of our ancestors.

TODAY'S TECHNOLOGY

Computers have now made it possible for Frith's many thousands of images to be accessed almost instantly. In the Frith archive today, each photograph is carefully 'digitised' then stored on a CD Rom. Frith archivists can locate a single photograph amongst thousands within seconds. Views can be catalogued and sorted under a variety of categories of place and content to the immediate benefit of researchers. Inexpensive reference prints can be created for them at the touch of a mouse button, and a wide range of books and other printed materials assembled and published for a wider, more general readership - in the next twelve months over a hundred Frith local history titles will be published! The

See Frith at www. frithbook.co.uk

day-to-day workings of the archive are very different from how they were in Francis Frith's time: imagine the herculean task of sorting through eleven tons of glass negatives as Frith had to do to locate a particular sequence of pictures! Yet the archive still prides itself on maintaining the same high standards of excellence laid down by Francis Frith, including the painstaking cataloguing and indexing of every view.

It is curious to reflect on how the internet now allows researchers in America and elsewhere greater instant access to the archive than Frith himself ever enjoyed. Many thousands of individual views can be called up on screen within seconds on one of the Frith internet sites, enabling people living continents away to revisit the streets of their ancestral home town, or view places in Britain where they have enjoyed holidays. Many overseas researchers welcome the chance to view special theme selections, such as transport, sports, costume and ancient monuments.

We are certain that Francis Frith would have heartily approved of these modern developments, for he himself was always working at the very limits of Victorian photographic technology.

THE VALUE OF THE ARCHIVE TODAY

Because of the benefits brought by the computer, Frith's images are increasingly studied by social historians, by researchers into genealogy and ancestory, by architects, town planners, and by teachers and schoolchildren involved in local history projects. In addition, the archive offers every one of us a unique opportunity to examine the places where we and our families have lived and worked down the years. Immensely successful in Frith's own era, the archive is now, a century and more on, entering a new phase of popularity.

THE PAST IN TUNE WITH THE FUTURE

Historians consider the Francis Frith Collection to be of prime national importance. It is the only archive of its kind remaining in private ownership and has been valued at a million pounds. However, this figure is now rapidly increasing as digital technology enables more and more people around the world to enjoy its benefits.

Francis Frith's archive is now housed in an historic timber barn in the beautiful village of Teffont in Wiltshire. Its founder would not recognize the archive office as it is today. In place of the many thousands of dusty boxes containing glass plate negatives and an all-pervading odour of photographic chemicals, there are now ranks of computer screens. He would be amazed to watch his images travelling round the world at unimaginable speeds through network and internet lines.

The archive's future is both bright and exciting. Francis Frith, with his unshakeable belief in making photographs available to the greatest number of people, would undoubtedly approve of what is being done today with his lifetime's work. His photographs, depicting our shared past, are now bringing pleasure and enlightenment to millions around the world a century and more after his death.

CAMBRIDGESHIRE – *An Introduction*

MODERN CAMBRIDGESHIRE ENCOM-PASSES not just the old county of the same name, but Huntingdonshire, the Isle of Ely and the Soke of Peterborough. The county is bounded to the north by Lincolnshire, to the east by Norfolk and Suffolk, to the south by Essex and Hertfordshire, and to the west by Bedfordshire and Northamptonshire. The greater part of it is flat - today's Fenland is probably the most fertile arable land in the country, and yet it has not reached this state without some considerable effort over a long period of time.

For hundreds of years, the Fens existed as wild and desolate mist-shrouded marshes, a wasteland of sedge and reeds, with outcrops of land forming 'islands', such as Ely, Thorney and Ramsey. In the summer, it was possible to graze sheep and cattle, and there were, of course, the proceeds from reed cutting, and some wildfowling. In the winter, the rivers overflowed, flooding the peaty countryside to such an extent that no agriculture was possible.

The Romans recognised the problem, and tried unsuccessfully to drain the land. When William the Conqueror invaded England,

most of it fell to his Norman soldiers fairly quickly. But in Fenland, a small pocket of resistance remained as a thorn in the Normans' sides for a good five years after the Conquest of 1066, and it was largely due to the inaccessible nature of the marshy terrain that Hereward managed to hold out for so long.

Hereward's name wasn't recorded as 'the Wake' until the latter part of the 14th century. It is presumed that it was taken from the Anglo-Saxon nickname meaning 'watchful'. His land-owning family originated from Bourne in Lincolnshire, but in 1062 he became an outlaw, and left England to try his luck in Flanders. After the invasion, William tried to consolidate his stranglehold by deposing the rich, powerful monasteries and other wealthy landowners. It was whilst protecting his family and estate that Hereward's brother was killed at Bourne, and this event brought Hereward home in search of revenge. In 1069, Hereward was party to the sacking of the Anglo-Saxon monastery at Peterborough; afterwards he sought refuge in the Isle of Ely, protected by the treacherous surrounding marshes. It was an ideal base from which to harry the enemy, and easy to defend.

The Normans made several unsuccessful attempts at besieging the Isle, which included trying to lay a causeway across a narrow stretch of fen, probably at Aldreth or Stuntney. They did break into Ely eventually, but Hereward managed to escape the considerable bloodshed and retribution that followed. What happened to him after that remains unclear, although he was reputedly buried in the Abbey grounds at Crowland. The clergyman Charles Kingsley (author of 'The Water Babies') wrote a novel about Hereward the Wake, on which most of the notions of him as a romantic hero are founded.

As for those mist-shrouded marshes, it was not until the 17th century that sufficient technology existed to enable someone to tackle the reclamation of the Fens. The Earl of Bedford owned about 20,000 acres of land near Whittlesey, and it was he, along with some others, who employed a Dutch engineer, Cornelius Vermuyden, to drain the

land. These were the so-called Adventurers, who 'adventured' capital to fund the drainage schemes in return for allotments of the reclaimed land. Vermuyden's first attempt was the Old Bedford River, seventy feet wide, and a straight cut from Earith to Denver. This twenty-one mile stretch by-passed the Great Ouse, and allowed water to drain to the sea more quickly. Summer use of the land was improved, but it still tended to flood during the winter months.

Drainage of the Fens did not happen without some resistance. There were many whose livelihoods were affected by the schemes - wildfowlers in particular. Their cause was championed by Oliver Cromwell, which earned him the mock title 'Lord of the Fens'. When the Civil War was over, Vermuyden returned to improve his original scheme by constructing another drainage cut called the New Bedford River. It was parallel to the first cut, never running more than one kilometre from the first. The strip of land between the two man-made rivers was called the Ouse

Washes, as this was allowed to flood during the winter. Sluices at Earith and Denver controlled the flow of water in times of flood, directing it from the mainstream of the New Bedford River into the slightly lower Old Bedford, from which it overflowed into the Washes. Modifications have been made since, but the basic drainage system remains.

to the level of the sea, the pumps have to work harder. By contrast, Wicken Fen, which is largely undrained and now preserved as a nature reserve, is higher than the surrounding land. Constant agriculture also depletes the soil, and eventually there will be nothing covering the underlying clay.

Huntingdonshire shares the Fen region,

Many other rivers received similar treatment, with straight drainage cuts like Forty Foot, Sixteen Foot and Middle Level Drains duplicating their courses. Natural drainage proved not to be enough. At the same time, water had to be pumped from the fields into the rivers, whose embankments are higher than the surrounding countryside. Windpumps were used in the old days, but modern diesel or electric pumps have taken over, discharging water into tidal rivers when the tide is going out, then closing the sluices to stop it flooding back when the tide turns.

But one problem with improving the drainage was the fact that the peat dried out, which resulted in its shrinking. And so as the peaty land of the Fens slowly sinks in relation

fringed with rolling hills and dales of rich agricultural land. The River Ouse was one of its big assets as a main route for trading, as well as providing the water and power necessary to produce paper. Without a doubt, the region's most famous son was Oliver Cromwell. He was born in Huntingdon in 1599, in a house in the main street. The grammar school which he and diarist Samuel Pepys attended is now a museum devoted to Cromwell and the Great Rebellion of 1640-1660. He spent a year at Cambridge University, in Sidney Sussex College, before completing his education in the Inns of Court in London.

Cromwell lived in Huntingdon until 1631, becoming Member of Parliament for the town in 1629. The Parliament was short-lived, and Charles I embarked on eleven years of 'tyrannical' rule. Cromwell was made Justice of the Peace in 1630, but took the job a little too seriously. He fell out with the Mayor, and shortly after moved to St Ives. In 1640, Charles I assembled Parliament again, attempting to raise money to fight the Scots, who were rebelling at his efforts to introduce the English Prayer Book into Scotland. Cromwell, a respected landowner who had already stood up to the King over the controversial draining of the Fens, became MP for Cambridge. He took his place in Westminster in what was to become known as the Short Parliament, because it lasted just three weeks. But by the end of the year, Charles recalled Parliament. This was the birth of the famous Long Parliament which lasted until 1660.

Of Cromwell, parliamentarian John Hampden commented: 'that slovenly fellow which you see before us will be one of the greatest men of England'. Indeed, Cromwell's strong views and forthright manner brought him to the fore very quickly; through the bitter struggles of the Civil War, he was to show himself to be the most able military leader of the Roundheads - some would say one of the most brilliant in English history. When war was declared, East Anglia supported the rebel Parliament, and it was in Cambridge that Cromwell set up the headquarters for his Eastern Association, recruiting and fundraising for the Parliamentary cause from Trinity College.

After defeating the King, Cromwell promoted his trial and execution, becoming Lord Lieutenant. He was asked by Parliament to assume the title of King, but his conscience would not let him do so; he took instead the title Lord Protector - King in all but name. His death in 1658 left a space which no-one else was capable of filling successfully, and in 1660 Charles II returned to restore the monarchy.

Cambridgeshire's two main centres are Cambridge and Peterborough. Cambridge developed as a place of importance because of its position on the Granta, or River Cam. It was at the head of a navigation, and the only crossing point for some considerable distance, hence Cam-bridge. So what started out as an ideal military position turned into an ideal one for trading. When the first college buildings began to appear in the 13th century, the town's position on the river allowed the extravagant use of stone not native to the area. The first college to be founded was Peterhouse, by Hugh de Balsam, the Bishop of Ely. Over the next couple of hundred years, more colleges were added, and their power grew. The University acquired the right to inspect weights and measures, in order that traders would not take advantage of the students, which in turn led to an uneasy relationship between 'town and gown'.

In the 15th century came the Royal College of the Blessed Virgin Mary and St Nicholas of Canterbury, subsequently known as King's College, founded by Henry VI. He had already set up Eton College in Windsor, and the new college would have its scholars drawn from there. As with Eton, his first concern was the establishment of a chapel. Its design would be modelled more on the lines of a cathedral choir rather than the buildings typical of college chapels so far - this was the reason why the King's master mason, Reginald of Ely, was appointed as architect. Building started in 1446, but came to a premature stop with the Wars of the Roses; after

Henry's death, it fell to Edward IV and Henry VII to continue the building, with Henry VIII overseeing the finishing touches in 1513. While monastic properties fell to Henry VIII's Reformation, the colleges of Cambridge remained secure. In fact the king even used the proceeds of dissolved religious establishments to set up his own college, when he merged Michaelhouse and King's Hall into Trinity College.

Once called Gildenburgh (or Golden Borough), Peterborough's riches were directly attributable to its monastery. Until the dissolution, the abbot exercised control over the area, and sheep farming provided a handsome income. The monastery then became the cathedral, a special dispensation on the part of Henry VIII. His first wife, Catherine of Aragon, was buried there, and he did not want the place to fall into disrepair. The general layout of the city is attributed to Martin de Vecti, who, as Abbot from 1133 to 1155, rebuilt the town on the western side of the

monastery, ensuring that its foundations lay in dry limestone rather than the often-flooded marshlands to the east. Abbot Martin was responsible for laying out the market place, and the wharf beside the river.

The cathedral is the focal point of the city, having risen from the monastery originally founded in 654 by Paeda, the king of Mercia. The present building is Norman, and is one of only three churches in Europe with an early painted wooden ceiling in its nave; of those three, Peterborough's is by far the biggest. Catherine of Aragon is buried in the North Choir Aisle, and Mary, Queen of Scots lay in the South Aisle for twenty-five years after her execution before being reinterred in Westminster Abbey. The portrait of Old Scarlett, the gravedigger who buried both queens, can be seen on the West wall. Up until the 1860s, it would have been possible to hail a sedan chair outside the cathedral gate. Peterborough was one of the last cities in the country to operate a sedan chair service.

CAMBRIDGE, KING'S PARADE 1933 85547

This photograph looks out onto King's Parade from the front of King's College. To the left is the Senate House, while the tower with four distinctive turrets belongs to the Church of Great St Mary. At the tailor's across the road, blazers are selling for 32/6 - £1.62 in today's money.

CAMBRIDGE, KING'S PARADE 1933 85551x

An Austin 'Chummy' 7, parked in King's Parade outside the gatehouse which leads into the Front Court of King's College, built in 1828 by William Wilkins. Beyond is the Chapel, unsurpassed in its magnificence, with the largest and most complete set of ancient windows in the world.

CAMBRIDGE, KING'S PARADE 1911 63639
Looking north along King's Parade, with the Senate
House in the distance, and the front of King's somewhat
obscured on the left. This is an interesting time as far as
the traffic is concerned, with a horse-drawn vehicle,
a motor car and bicycles all in the same view.

CAMBRIDGE, KING'S PARADE 1890 26496
Hansom cabs line up in King's Parade, outside the elegant classically designed Senate House to the right. Designed by James Gibbs, it is the meeting place of the governing body of the University, and the place where degrees are conferred. The impressive King's College Chapel is to the left.

CAMBRIDGE, KING'S COLLEGE 1909 61480
The Backs, which are the lawns, meadows and gardens behind the colleges which back on to the River Cam, are a favourite place for recreation. In the foreground, some young ladies appear to be trying their hands at rowing, whilst midstream we have what is more commonly associated with the river in Cambridge: punters.

CAMBRIDGE, ST JOHN'S COLLEGE 1890 26443
Here we see St John's College Old Bridge, originally conceived by Wren, but brought into being in 1712 by Robert Grumbold. Just beyond, joining Third and New Courts of St John's College, is the Bridge of Sighs, its Gothic design unashamedly borrowed from the covered bridge of the same name in Venice.

CAMBRIDGE, ST JOHN'S COLLEGE OLD BRIDGE 1890 26454
The Old Bridge is seen this time from the Bridge of Sighs. Beyond is the Wren Library, part of Trinity College.

CAMBRIDGE, ST JOHN'S COLLEGE 1890 26449A

CAMBRIDGE
St John's College 1890
Joining the two courts of St John's College on either side of the River Cam is the Bridge of Sighs. It borrows the idea of the covered bridge from one of the same name in Venice. Although the Cambridge version, built in 1831, has barred unglazed windows, the students passing through it were not necessarily looking their last upon the outside world as were the users of the original!

◆

CAMBRIDGE
Peterhouse 1890
Peterhouse is distinguished as Cambridge's first college, although the original 13th century buildings have been altered considerably. Matthew Wren (uncle of the more famous Christopher) was master here from 1625-34, and he was responsible for the chapel, which combines Perpendicular and classical styles.

CAMBRIDGE, PETERHOUSE 1890 26585

CAMBRIDGE, SUSSEX STREET 1938 88523

Sussex Street, running between Sidney and Hobson Streets, was redeveloped in the 1930s and finished off with these elegant colonnades. In recent years, the buildings at the far end of the street have been joined by a section which forms an archway.

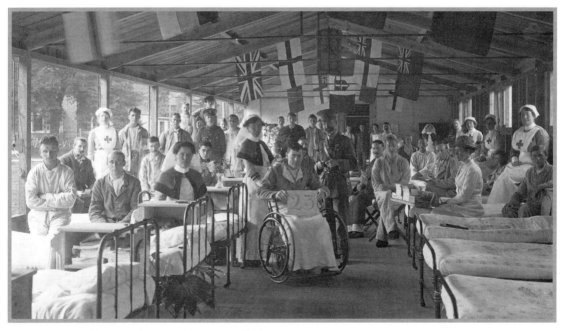

CAMBRIDGE, 1ST EASTERN GENERAL HOSPITAL C1920 C14701

The 1st Eastern General Hospital was set up in Nevile's Court in Trinity College at the beginning of World War 1, with beds placed around the cloisters. As more and more injured men came back from the front, a larger hut hospital was built on the playing fields of King's and Clare Colleges, with 'open-air' wards such as this one housing the patients.

CAMBRIDGE, ST ANDREW'S STREET 1908 60871

On the right-hand side of the road is First Court, the entrance to Christ's College, founded in 1505 by Lady Margaret Beaufort, mother of Henry VII. On the other side of the road is the church of St Andrew the Great, which contains a monument to the explorer Captain Cook, along with the graves of his widow and two sons, the younger of whom attended Christ's College until he died of scarlet fever.

CAMBRIDGE, CHRIST'S COLLEGE 1908 60831

A hansom cab waits for a fare outside the entrance to Christ's College in 1908. Founded by Henry VII's mother, Margaret Beaufort (as was St John's), the impressive gateway depicts her coat of arms, with a statue of her above. In the college gardens stands a mulberry tree under which Milton is said to have written Lycidas.

CAMBRIDGE, MARKET PLACE 1890 26617

Perhaps it is not on a par with the great Suffolk wool churches, but Great St Mary's, overlooking the Market Place, is none the less an impressive piece of Perpendicular architecture. Many great clerics have preached here, including Latimer, Ridley and Cranmer.

CAMBRIDGE, PETTY CURY 1909 61469
Even at the turn of the century, there is no doubt that Cambridge had traffic problems, with horse-drawn carriages and bicycles filling this bustling thoroughfare.

CAMBRIDGE, HOBBS' PAVILION 1931 84523

Born in Cambridge in 1882, Sir John Berry 'Jack' Hobbs was undoubtedly the world's greatest cricket batsman of his time. Between 1905 and 1934 he played in 61 test matches and scored a record 61,237 runs. Perhaps his greatest innings at the Oval was against Australia in 1926, when he made a century to help bring back the Ashes to England. Hobbs' Pavilion on Parker's Piece (note the batsman wind vane) honours Cambridge's sporting son. These days, Hobbs' Pavilion is a restaurant.

CAMBRIDGE, PEMBROKE COLLEGE 1890 26553

Pembroke College was founded in 1347, and is significant in that it was here that Christopher Wren first translated a design from the drawing board into stone. It was commissioned by Wren's uncle, the Bishop of Ely, who after spending eighteen years in prison, decided that a building would be a fitting way to celebrate his release!

CAMBRIDGE, EIGHTS 1909 61510

Cambridge has a long history of rowing. The River Cam itself is not wide enough for conventional races, so races called 'Bumps' are held. Eights such as this one start off about one and a half lengths behind one another, and each boat has to catch up with the one in front, thus 'bumping' it.

CAMBRIDGE, GIRTON COLLEGE 1938 88501

Cambridge's first women's college started out in Hitchin in 1869, and moved to Girton three years later - sufficiently far removed from Cambridge and the temptations of its male students. But while these red-brick buildings offered women a higher education, it was to be another twenty years before women became entitled to receive degrees.

IMPINGTON, THE CHURCH c1965 H442011

As with so many churches, St Andrew's in Impington exhibits an interesting blend of styles. The chancel was extensively rebuilt in the latter part of the 19th century, but the rest is considerably older, including the timber-framed porch, which dates back to late medieval times.

GRANTCHESTER, THE CHURCH 1929 81771

The last two lines of Rupert Brooke's poem 'The Old Vicarage, Grantchester' have immortalised the church: 'Stands the church clock at ten to three/And is there honey still for tea?' It is believed that the clock was actually broken when the poet was living in Grantchester. For years after Brooke's death, the clock was kept at that time as a memorial to him.

GRANTCHESTER
The Old Mill 1914

'And laughs the immortal river still/Under the mill, under the mill'. So wrote the poet Rupert Brooke about Grantchester's mill. The river may well be immortal, but the mill certainly was not. It burned down in 1928.

◆

MADINGLEY
The Church c1955

Madingley is a typical example of an estate village, remodelled in order to improve the view from the landlord's mansion. When the Cotton family commissioned Capability Brown to design a park in 1756, he cut a swathe through the village, separating the church and a couple of farms and cottages from the rest of the village.

GRANTCHESTER, THE OLD MILL 1914 66908A

MADINGLEY, THE CHURCH c1955 M5006

MADINGLEY, THE RUINED WINDMILL 1909 61524

MADINGLEY
The Ruined Windmill 1909
Looking very much a shadow of its former self, this windmill would have ground corn. In common with other mills in the area, it is a post mill, with the mill revolving round the central post.

◆

TRUMPINGTON
The Village 1914
A set of stone steps leading nowhere might seem a rather odd thing to have on the roadside. They were, of course, designed to make life easier when using transport of the four-legged variety, even though by the time this photograph was taken the motor car was beginning to make its presence felt.

TRUMPINGTON, THE VILLAGE 1914 66916

TRUMPINGTON, THE VILLAGE 1914 66910
Thatched cottages abound in this view of Trumpington. At this time, the village was separate from Cambridge.
Although only visible from its sign in this picture, the Green Man is a magnificent timbered public house.

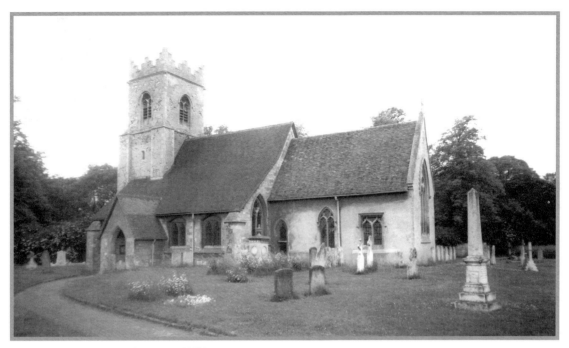

TEVERSHAM, ALL SAINTS CHURCH c1965 T298001
This photograph shows the tranquillity of the churchyard in Teversham, just a stone's throw from the bustle of nearby Cambridge. The church's Jacobean pulpit came from the neighbouring parish church in Cherry Hinton.

TEVERSHAM, HIGH STREET c1965 T298004
Post-war expansion of Cambridge pushed the suburbs into outlying villages. We can see early signs of the requirement to control traffic flow with the now ubiquitous Keep Left bollards.

FULBOURN, HIGH STREET c1950 F104008

One hopes that the Express parcel service fared better than the shop's window advertising, which suffers from a number of missing letters! In the background is the Six Bells public house, while to the left, the church is one of only two in England dedicated to Saint Vigor.

FULBOURN, HIGH STREET c1950 F104002

Peering just around the corner of the house on the right is a petrol pump. This might have been quite acceptable in the 1950s perhaps, but not legal now.

FEN DITTON, THE CHURCH 1914 66915
An early tractor makes its way past the church. The village lies along the line of Fleam Dyke, an ancient
defensive earthwork.

GREAT SHELFORD, WOOLLARDS LANE c1955 G278013
We see typical fifties fashion here with the boy's open shirt collar worn over his jacket collar. Note too the bicycle
parked on the other side of the road, with the pedal set back on the kerb so it can act as a stand.

GREAT SHELFORD, WOOLLARDS LANE c1955 G278012
The cyclists here obviously felt sufficiently safe not to worry too much about hugging the kerb and avoiding brushes with the traffic. The practice of parking a bicycle by leaning it on one pedal against the kerb is rarely seen these days.

LITTLE SHELFORD, KING'S MILL LANE c1955 L460004
A picture of wonderful rural character, with cottages and barns with thatched roofs, and spring blossom appearing on the trees. All Saints church tower can just be seen on the far right.

LINTON
The Clapper Stile c1955
This little lad demonstrates the ingenuity of a stile which maintains the integrity of the field boundary without the need for steps over the fence. Simply push the three rails down, and step over! This one is the only example of a clapper stile in Cambridgeshire.

◆

LINTON
The Church c1955
This view shows Church Street, with St Mary's church on the left, the 16th-century timber-framed Trinity Guildhall in the foreground, and a charming plastered and thatched cottage in between.

LINTON, THE CLAPPER STILE c1955 L459012

LINTON, THE CHURCH c1955 L459076

LINTON, HIGH STREET c1955 L459025
Linton had a regular market from the Middle Ages, and it was the last place outside Cambridge to maintain one, but it came to an end around 1860, supplanted by its shops.

LINTON, THE VILLAGE c1955 L459028
This photograph was taken just a few steps on along the High Street from photograph No L459025.

LINTON, OLD COTTAGES c1955 L459041
Thatch and pantile-roofed cottages like these are timber-framed with clay lump infill. The clay, dug out close by, and generally leaving a pond in its wake, will be mixed with straw and then either moulded into blocks or poured straight into shuttering to make the walls. The outside is then rendered to protect it from the weather.

BALSHAM, THE POST OFFICE AND STORES c1955 B725002
Balsham is situated at the opposite end of Fleam Dyke to Fulbourn. Fleam Dyke is a three mile long earthwork built in the 7th century to defend East Anglia from the Mercians.

BALSHAM, CAMBRIDGE ROAD c1955 B725013

Enamelled metal advertising signs, much sought after as collector's items these days, abound on the walls of this little village shop.

DULLINGHAM, CROSS GREEN c1955 D206006

The main part of Dullingham village lies along the southern edge of the grounds of the early 18th-century Dullingham House, hence the picturesque thatched estate cottages.

SWAFFHAM BULBECK, THE VILLAGE GREEN c1955 S678001
Swaffham Bulbeck's vicar for much of the 19th century was Leonard Blomefield, alias Jenyns. He was a close friend of Charles Darwin, and they both used to go on nature rambles together. It was Jenyns, in fact, who gave up his place on the Beagle to allow Darwin to go instead.

BOTTISHAM, HIGH STREET c1955 B727008
Bottisham seems to have had more than its fair share of bad luck over the ages. In 1712 twenty houses were destroyed in a fire. Then, in February 1846, fire destroyed the produce of two large farms, as well as fifteen cottages. Twenty-four families lost their homes.

WATERBEACH
Bottisham Lock, River Cam c1955
Here we see manually-operated lock gates in the River Cam at Waterbeach, north of Cambridge. These days the lock is electrically operated.

◆

HORNINGSEA
The Village c1955
Attractive thatched and pantile-roofed houses line the street, the skyline softened by the mature trees on the left-hand side. Not so attractive, though doubtless functional, is that typical example of post-war village architecture, the bus shelter.

WATERBEACH, BOTTISHAM LOCK, RIVER CAM c1955 W509009

HORNINGSEA, THE VILLAGE c1955 H443004

WILLINGHAM, THE POST OFFICE c1960 W510304
The distinctive ash-framed Morris Traveller, the estate version of the Morris Minor, is parked outside the post office and general stores in Willingham. Note the bubble gum machine on the wall next to the door.

WILLINGHAM, CHURCH STREET c1955 W510010

Situated on the edge of the Fens, Wilingham is a typical example of the 'shoreline' villages that prospered through their access to better grazing for their sheep. The superb church has a hammerbeam roof almost as perfect as the one at March.

SAWSTON, ST MARY'S CHURCH c1965 S671007

The lofty-aisled Norman nave of St Mary's was extended in the 13th century. It was at nearby Sawston Hall that Mary Tudor spent a night with the Huddleston family in 1553.

HINXTON, THE RED LION c1960 H441016

HINXTON
The Red Lion c1960
Very few changes have been made to this attractive 16th-century coaching inn since the photograph was taken. The chimney stack in the foreground has been removed, and the building has been extended at the back. The main bar is dominated by a central fireplace with built-in bread oven.

HINXTON
The Mill and the River c1960
The 17th-century mill at Hinxton oozes character with its weatherboarded walls, although the corrugated asbestos roof it sports in this view does not particularly add to its charms. In recent years, it has been restored to full working order.

HINXTON, THE MILL AND THE RIVER c1960 H441007

MELBOURN, HIGH STREET c1965 M301006

Here we see an attractive row of thatched cottages on Melbourn's High Street. Not far from here is Bran Ditch, a defensive earthworks in which the skeletons of Romano-British soldiers have been discovered.

MELDRETH, FENNY LANE c1965 M302012

From medieval times until the early 19th century, Meldreth consisted of several small communities scattered along a two-mile stretch of winding road. During the rest of the 19th century, the population doubled, turning the village into a continuous linear settlement.

BOURN, BOURN MILL c1955 B713009

BOURN
Bourn Mill c1955

Just a windmill, you might think, but this dark weatherboarded post mill is the oldest of its type in the country, dating back to around 1620 or possibly earlier.

BOURN
High Street c1955

Charming thatched cottages on Bourn's High Street. These days, Bourn is probably best known for Bourn Hall clinic, renowned the world over for its pioneering work with test-tube babies. The hall itself, an Elizabethan mansion, was built on the site of a former castle built by the Sheriff of Cambridgeshire after the Norman conquest.

BOURN, HIGH STREET c1955 B713006

ELY

The Cathedral c1878

The west end of Ely Cathedral was once symmetrical until the northern part collapsed in the 15th century. The porch is known as the Galilee porch, so called because as Galilee was the furthest place in the Holy Land from Bethlehem, so too is the west porch furthest from the altar. The cannon on Palace Green in the foreground is Russian, captured during the Crimean War.

ELY

Market Place 1925

While the cathedral is the main feature of Ely, the town has also been a market town for many years. At the time this photograph was taken, the Market Place occupied far more space than it does these days.

ELY, THE CATHEDRAL c1878 10956

ELY, MARKET PLACE 1925 78276

ELY, FORE HILL c1955 E34007
A view of Fore Hill, an attractive street which
continues from the High Street, descending to the
River Ouse. Although the town itself is very much
low-key compared to the impressive cathedral, it does
have its place in folklore, with its association with
Hereward the Wake; it is more firmly rooted in history
through its connection with Oliver Cromwell, for a
time Member of Parliament for Ely.

SOHAM, FROM THE CHURCH TOWER c1955 S597002
Soham's 15th century church tower is an imposing landmark throughout the surrounding fens, so it is not surprising that it also makes a good viewpoint. Between Soham and Wicken once lay a large expanse of water called Soham Mere. It suffered from gradual encroachment by farmers over the centuries, and finally succumbed in the drainage of 1664.

SOHAM, HIGH STREET c1955 S597009
The monastery founded here in the 7th century by St Felix rivalled Ely until its destruction by the Danes in 870. Even so, it retained its importance, standing on one of the two causeways to Ely.

SOHAM, THE STEELYARD C1955 S597004
Soham's 17th century steelyard is attached to the back of the Fountain Inn. It was used for weighing the wagonloads of produce on their way to the market. When it was overhauled in 1929, it was found to be accurate to within two ounces!

WICKEN, THE POND c1955 W493002
Reed-thatched cottages abound in the pretty village of Wicken. Nearby Wicken Fen is virtually the only remaining piece of natural undrained Fenland left. It was the first nature reserve to be set up by the National Trust, in 1899.

BURWELL, HIGH STREET c1955 B728031
There is no hint of a dark secret in this view. But in 1727, a company of players gave a performance in a nearby barn. So popular was it, that the doors were nailed shut to prevent any more people from getting in. But then a fire started, and eighty-two people were burned to death. Nearly fifty years later, an old man on his deathbed confessed to having caused this terrible tragedy. A monument to the dead stands in Burwell's churchyard.

BURWELL, THE MILL c1955 B728009H
When this photograph was taken, the tower mill which overlooks Burwell was still fully functioning. The last remaining windpump in Cambridgeshire was taken from nearby Adventurer's Fen and resited at Wicken Fen in 1956.

SUTTON, THE VILLAGE AND THE CHURCH c1955 S674001
Sutton's church was started in 1366 by Bishop Barnett of Ely, and the octagon - in fact, two octagons, one on top of the other - was doubtless inspired by the octagon adorning Ely Cathedral.

EARITH, THE SUSPENSION BRIDGE c1955 E201010
Earith is where the two great drainage cuts of Fenland, the Old and New Bedford Rivers, take off from the Great Ouse. The drains run north-east, roughly parallel for approximately twenty miles. During the winter, the strip of land known as the Ouse Washes in between is allowed to flood, and is consequently a major haven for wildlife.

EARITH
High Street c1955 E201003
It was in Victorian times on the Old Bedford River near Earith
that a most bizarre experiment took place. A wager had been
placed on whether or not the earth was flat, and the Old
Bedford River was chosen to prove or disprove the theory, as it
was the longest, straightest stretch of calm water in the country.
The experiment was performed using three boats with masts of
equal height moored along the length of the river. When
sighted through a telescope, the masts were found not to be in
line, and the Flat-Earther who had instigated the experiment
was discredited.

EARITH, SEVEN HOLES BRIDGE c1955 E201305
This aptly-named bridge is actually a sluice, controlling the water level in the Old Bedford River.

BLUNTISHAM, HIGH STREET c1955 B726015
Without doubt, Bluntisham's most famous daughter was the novellist Dorothy L Sayers, creator of the famous detective Lord Peter Wimsey. Her father was rector at Bluntisham, and she spent most of her childhood here.

SOMERSHAM, THE CROSS c1955 S672005

Somersham stretches for about a mile along a kink in the road between St Ives and Chatteris. The village was once celebrated for its mineral spa.

CHATTERIS, HIGH STREET c1955 C210011

It is the mid 1950's, the early days of television. Bearing in mind the fact that you cannot get much flatter than Fenland, just look at the height of the TV aerials!

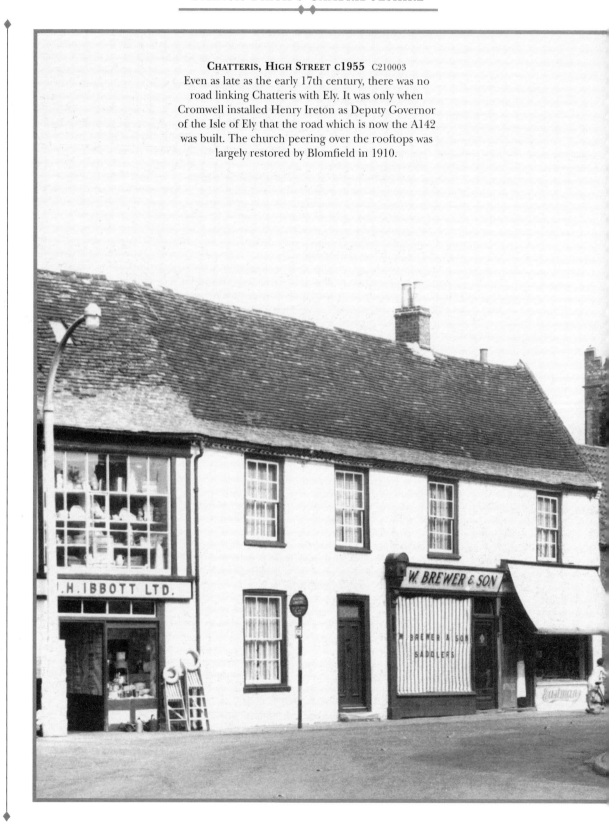

CHATTERIS, HIGH STREET c1955 C210003
Even as late as the early 17th century, there was no road linking Chatteris with Ely. It was only when Cromwell installed Henry Ireton as Deputy Governor of the Isle of Ely that the road which is now the A142 was built. The church peering over the rooftops was largely restored by Blomfield in 1910.

WARBOYS, JUBILEE CLOCK AND SQUARE c1955 W508010
This impressive clock tower was erected in the Square in 1887 to commemorate Queen Victoria's Golden Jubilee. It cost the parishioners of Warboys £200.

WARBOYS, THE CHURCH c1955 W508002
Here we see Warboys church, with the 17th-century Dutch-influenced manor house next door. The village is renowned as the scene of a notorious Elizabethan witch hunt, when 80 year old Alice Samuel called on a neighbour whose child was ill. The child accused her of witchcraft, a charge repeated by four sisters, and ultimately by Lady Cromwell, who died. Alice Samuel, with her husband and daughter, were arrested and tried in Huntingdon. They were found guilty of witchcraft and hanged in 1593.

RAMSEY, HIGH STREET c1955 R359017

Ramsey attained early importance with the foundation of its abbey in 969. It survived for around five hundred years until Henry VIII's dissolution of the monasteries in the 16th century. These days, Ramsey is one of the smallest towns in England to have its own mayor, and all that remains of the abbey is one gatehouse.

RAMSEY, GREAT WHYTE c1955 R359026

Up until just over a hundred years ago, a watercourse, or lode, ran down the centre of this street. Cut from the Old Nene river around two miles away, its purpose was to allow access to boats supplying goods to the town and abbey.

PETERBOROUGH, MARKET PLACE AND CATHEDRAL 1904 51544
This view shows the west front of the Cathedral, with a tram
crossing the Market Place in front. Note the shutters covering
the windows of Burlingham's watchmakers and jewellers.

PETERBOROUGH, COWGATE 1904 51559
Here, we are looking along Cowgate towards the market place. Just out of sight is the magnificent 17th-century Guildhall, supported by columns to provide an open ground floor.

PETERBOROUGH, THE CATHEDRAL FROM THE SOUTH-EAST 1890 24436
The cathedral rose from the monastery originally founded in 654 by Paeda, the king of Mercia. The present building is Norman, and is one of only three churches in Europe with an early painted wooden ceiling in its nave; of those three, Peterborough's is by far the biggest.

PETERBOROUGH, THE RIVER NENE 1952 P47041
Houses from a bygone era are set against the less attractive backdrop of more modern industry. Although the majority of the boats in the picture are pleasure boats, the River Nene is still an important route for the carriage of goods.

MARCH, MARKET PLACE c1955 M28046
Back in 1900, Kelly's Directory of Cambridgeshire said of March's Market Place:
'the Fire Engine House is in the Market Place; there is one 40 horse power steam engine by Shand and Mason, with about half-a-mile of leather and canvas hose'.

MARCH, THE BRIDGE FROM NENE QUAY 1929 81913
The town's name comes from the Anglo-Saxon word for frontier or border. March stood on the line between Middle Anglia and East Anglia, with trade built up on the fishing or trading based on the Fenland rivers. By medieval times, March was a thriving town with an influence way beyond its bounds.

MARCH, HIGH STREET c1955 M28036

One senses a certain interaction taking place in this photograph. The boy on the left appears to have been diverted from what he was doing: probably he has been hailed by the two cyclists opposite Lloyd's Bank, who seem to be about to head across the road towards him.

MARCH, BROAD STREET c1955 M28001

A fine summer's day in March! With fewer cars on the road, cycling was a good deal safer. The woman with the pram is using a pedestrian crossing marked with belisha beacons, yellow globes flashing on and off atop black and white striped poles - these had been instituted some twenty years previously, when Leslie Hore-Belisha was Minister of Transport.

MARCH, HIGH STREET 1929 81909
Evidently it was a hot summer's day when this photograph was taken. The butcher's on the right-hand side of the road is taking every precaution to keep the temperature down inside his shop.

March, St Wendreda's Church 1929 81922

The roof of St Wendreda's Church is a testament to the carpenter's art, a hammerbeam roof with one hundred and twenty angels playing musical instruments. Tradition has it that it survived the destruction wrought during Henry VIII's Reformation because the townspeople treated the Commissioners to a marvellous feast - which quite obviously took the wind out of their sails!

WISBECH ST MARY, THE STORES C1960 W492009

An interesting jumble of crates and old carpet vie for space with the advertising in front of this shop selling general stores and provisions.

LEVERINGTON, THE VILLAGE C1965 L451009

There's no doubt that cycling like this today would be courting disaster! Leverington's church, dedicated to St Leonard, was founded in the 12th century. The building which stands now was built somewhat later, and is distinguished as a piece of particularly fine architecture.

WISBECH, THE MARKET 1929 81976
Wisbech's elongated market place bustles with
activity on Thursdays and Saturdays. Peering
over the rooftops on the right-hand side is the
solid 16th-century tower of the church of St
Peter and St Paul, built of stone
from Northamptonshire.

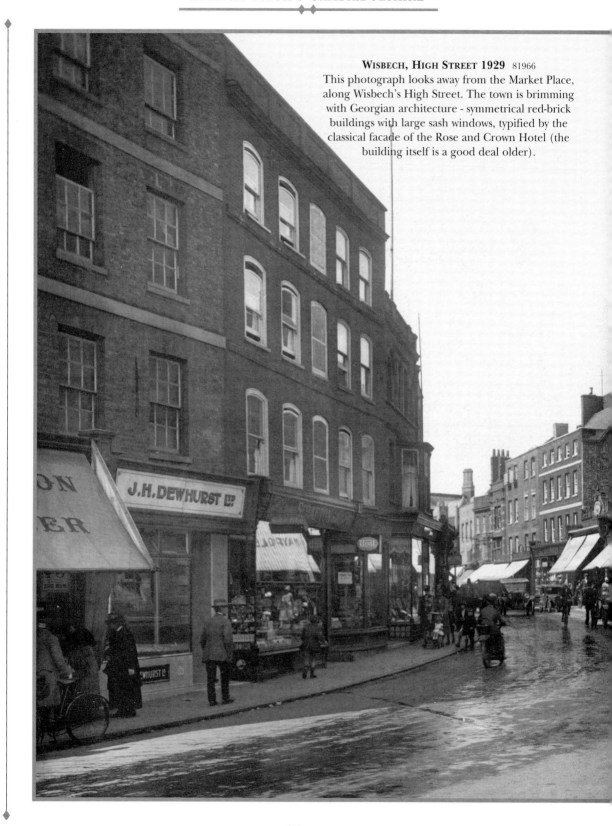

WISBECH, HIGH STREET 1929 81966
This photograph looks away from the Market Place, along Wisbech's High Street. The town is brimming with Georgian architecture - symmetrical red-brick buildings with large sash windows, typified by the classical facade of the Rose and Crown Hotel (the building itself is a good deal older).

WISBECH, THE CLARKSON MEMORIAL 1901 47583

This splendid sixty-eight feet high Gothic-style memorial beside the old bridge in Wisbech is to Thomas Clarkson, who dedicated his life to travelling the country, speaking in support of William Wilberforce's anti-slavery movement. Unveiled in 1881, the monument was designed by Sir Gilbert Scott, and contains bas-relief panels created by Josiah Wedgwood.

WISBECH, VIEW FROM NORTH BRINK 1901 47584

Although it is 10 miles from the sea on what is now an artificial River Nene, Wisbech maintains its long tradition as a sea port. It is the wealth created by the years of shipping which has given Wisbech two of the most perfect Georgian streets in England - the Brinks. The North and South Brinks, sombre rows of mansions and warehouses, look out over each other on opposite sides of the river.

ELM, THE VILLAGE 1923 73583

Here we see the village green in Elm, with its recently erected memorial to the men of the village who fell in the Great War. The village's name was spelt 'Eolum' around a thousand years ago, so the name possibly means a place of eels rather than elm trees.

UPWELL, THE VILLAGE 1923 73591

The Old Ouse river runs through both Upwell and Outwell, the next village downstream. The county boundary between Cambridgeshire and Norfolk actually runs along the middle of the river at this point, so the church is in Norfolk, while the pub is in Cambridgeshire!

LITTLEPORT, THE RIVER c1955 L366006
Maintaining safe navigation along the River Great Ouse is an ongoing task, which means dredging to ensure there is no build-up of silt.

LITTLEPORT, MAIN STREET c1955 L366010
Littleport is distinguished as being the last place on which the Bishop of Ely exercised his temporal powers. In 1816, local farm workers, enraged at being made unemployed as a result of the enclosure of common land, marched to Ely and caused a disturbance. The Bishop called in the army, and appointed judges to make an example of the rioters. Five were hanged, and many others were transported.

OVER, THE CHURCH c1965 O114004

Situated on the Great Ouse (Over actually means 'river bank'), the church of St Mary is lavishly built from Barnack stone, with an ornately decorated interior, and stone seats extending around much of the walls. There is also much lovely woodwork within, with misericords reputedly from Ramsey Abbey.

HOLYWELL, THE FERRY 1914 66972

Here we see the chain ferry across the Great Ouse at Holywell. On the far shore is the renowned Ferry Boat Inn, which has been selling beer since 1068 - in fact there are documents which suggest it was an inn as early as 980, which makes it one of the oldest licensed houses in the country.

HOLYWELL, THE VILLAGE 1914 66970

Seen here from the other side is the thatched Ferry Boat inn. Nearby is the grave of Juliet Tewsley, who hanged herself from a tree by the river because the woodcutter for whom she was waiting with a bunch of flowers stood her up! Reputedly her ghost walks on St Patrick's Day, and undoubtedly if you drink enough, you may see her too!

HOLYWELL, THE VILLAGE 1914 66968

The village takes its name from the well on the south side of the churchyard. It gained importance from the ferry which it operated over the Ouse to Fen Drayton.

St Ives, Market Hill and the Church 1901 48066

In the 13th century, St Ives was one of the biggest markets in Europe. Since then, encroachment by buildings greatly reduced its size. The statue is of the town's most famous resident, Oliver Cromwell, who lived here for five years in the 1630s. To his right is the Free Church, built in 1863 by the owner of a nearby flour mill.

St Ives, The Bridge 1899 44244

The bridge across the Ouse at St Ives was built in medieval times. Part of it was destroyed and a drawbridge put in its place as a defensive measure during the Civil War; it was then subsequently rebuilt. Its distinguishing feature - almost uniquely - is the chapel in the middle. The two upper storeys were added in 1736, and for a time the building was used as a public house. It was restored in 1929 when the upper storeys were demolished.

ST IVES, BRIDGE STREET 1914 66957
The building with the jettied gables to the left dates
back to the 17th century, on the face of it one of the
oldest buildings in St Ives, although earlier buildings
survive behind more modern facades. The buildings
on the right-hand side of the street have mainly
Georgian frontages.

ST IVES, CROMWELL'S BARN 1931 84558
Cromwell's family farmed at Slepe Hall in St Ives, but by all accounts they were not particularly successful at it; they were even thought to have contemplated emigrating to America at one point. As one observer said of Cromwell, 'he farmed here until he was very poor'.

ST IVES, OLD RIVER 1914 66958
Although the railways were well established by the start of the First World War, barges such as these still did plenty of trade carrying grain and other goods along the Fenland waterways.

St Ives, The Sheep Market 1931 84547

The region's strong agricultural tradition is reflected in this view of livestock at market. Note the dog jumping the railings in the middle of the picture.

St Ives, Market Day 1931 84549

Away from the livestock, on the other side of the recently erected war memorial, stalls sell everything from clothing and locally-grown produce to tractors and harrows.

ST IVES, MARKET SQUARE 1898 41279
The market here dates back to medieval times, when it
was one of the most important in existence. A great
fire in 1689 destroyed over a hundred houses. The
one thing that is missing in this view is the statue of
Oliver Cromwell outside the Free Church - it was
erected some three years after this photograph.

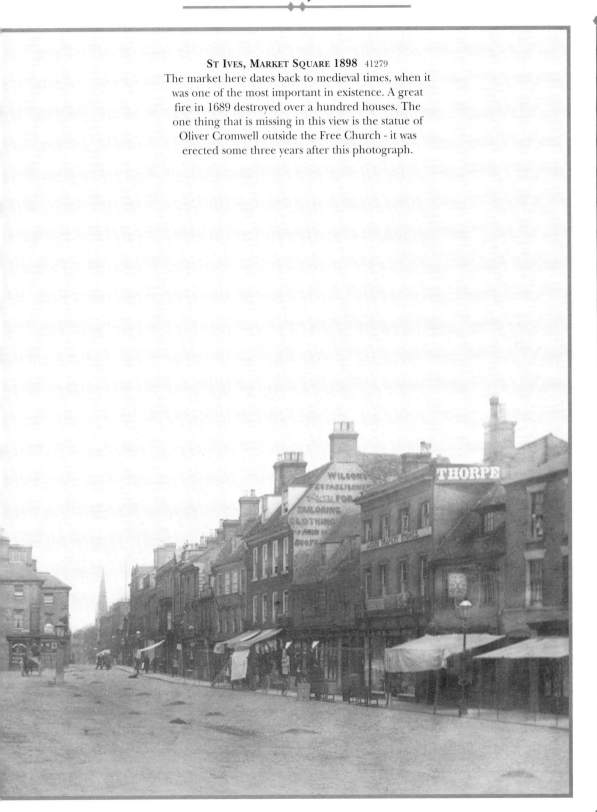

FENSTANTON, CHURCH LANE c1955 F191009
There is a somewhat run-down look in this view. Inside the church (not visible in this photograph) lies the tomb of Capability Brown, who became a cult figure among the aristocracy for his stylised landscaping. He was presented with the manors of Fenstanton and Hilton by the Earl of Northampton in payment for work at Castle Ashby.

HEMINGFORD GREY, ST JAMES' CHURCH 1898 41288
This delightful backwater of the Great Ouse is about as charming as you can get. The church is mostly medieval, and the unusual truncated style of its spire is the result of a hurricane in 1741. The debris from the spire is said still to lie on the river bed.

HILTON
The Church c1955

Next to Hilton's lovely church is the village green, landscaped by Capability Brown, and surrounded by houses dating back to Tudor times. Hilton sports a turf-cut maze as its most unusual feature.

◆

HEMINGFORD ABBOTS
From the River 1899

Until the 13th century, Huntingdon was a port on the River Great Ouse. Then the powerful Abbot of Ramsey built a weir across the river on his land at Hemingford Abbots, and he persuaded the Lord of neighbouring Hemingford Grey to do likewise. The explanation was to harness the river to drive watermills, but the real reason was to block navigation to Huntingdon, and increase their own rents and tolls from St Ives, which then became the head of navigation in the river.

HILTON, THE CHURCH C1955 H440001

HEMINGFORD ABBOTS, FROM THE RIVER 1899 44253

HEMINGFORD ABBOTS, THE VILLAGE 1914 66964

Hemingford Abbots is an attractive collection of brick, timbered and thatched cottages and houses, which originally started as just a small hamlet gathered around the church, but which subsequently grew westwards, towards Godmanchester.

HOUGHTON, THE MILL 1899 44257

A mill has stood on this site for over a thousand years. It was owned by the Benedictine monks at nearby Ramsey Abbey, whom the local farmers tended to regard as crooks. The Abbey was landlord to the local farmers, and had the power to insist they brought their grain here to be milled - they were fined if they didn't! The present brick and timber mill with tarred weatherboard cladding dates back to the 17th century.

HOUGHTON, THE VILLAGE 1914 66963
The thatched cottage in the foreground has a distinctly Dutch look to it - hardly surprising, given that an army of Dutchmen under Cornelius Vermuyden was responsible for draining the Fens in the 17th century. The end of the street opens out into the village square, complete with pump and clock, and overlooked (though not in this picture) by the church.

GODMANCHESTER, THE CHINESE BRIDGE 1898 41268
This beautiful wooden trellised bridge crosses the end of a mill stream, where it joins the River Ouse. It was built in 1827, but it has been rebuilt twice, most recently in 1960.

GODMANCHESTER, THE CHINESE BRIDGE c1955   G24043

GODMANCHESTER
The Chinese Bridge c1955
Seen here nearly sixty years after
photograph No 41268, this close-up
reveals the delicate trellis work which
makes the bridge such an attractive
feature of the town.

GODMANCHESTER
The Causeway c1955
This view shows a picturesque mix of
house styles, the timber-framed
examples probably dating from the early
17th century, fronting onto a pool,
essentially an inlet of the River Ouse.

GODMANCHESTER, THE CAUSEWAY c1955   G24014

HARTFORD, THE RIVER AND THE ANCHOR INN 1907 58555
Hartford lies between Huntingdon and St Ives, bordering on the Ouse. Much development has taken place in the late 20th century; but when this photograph was taken, the situation was picturesque indeed.

HUNTINGDON, THE BRIDGE 1898 41251
The medieval bridge over the River Ouse was started in 1332 to connect Huntingdon with Godmanchester, and the respective authorities paid for three arches - note the different styles - with the builders starting on each bank and meeting in the middle!

HUNTINGDON, HIGH STREET AND ST MARY'S CHURCH 1906 55420
The corners of the squat tower of St Mary's are adorned with ornate
buttresses. The lower part of the tower is medieval; the upper part
was rebuilt after it collapsed in 1608.

HUNTINGDON, THE BRIDGE FROM CASTLE HILL 1898 41252
The sturdy building on the opposite bank of the river was put up in the 1850s as a flour mill; later it was used for textiles. After a period of dereliction, it was converted into apartments.

HUNTINGDON, FROM THE RIVER 1898 41250
Huntingdon's two churches are visible in this picture; to the right is All Saints, with its spire, and the stumpy tower of St Mary's is to the left. In the foreground, a gardener tends his allotment.

HUNTINGDON, HIGH STREET 1901 46619
When this photograph was taken, there was not a lot more to Huntingdon than its long High Street, which leads
off Market Hill in both directions, overlooked by the graceful spire of All Saints.

HUNTINGDON, THE FOUNTAIN HOTEL 1906 55422
Although old coaching inns like the Fountain would have lost a certain amount of long-distance business with the development of the railways, they were still used as the pick-up and set-down points for carriages running the local 'bus' services. Next door, one of the early chain stores - Freeman, Hardy & Willis - has a window display which intriguingly blends the elaborate with the chaotic.

HUNTINGDON, THE OLD BRIDGE 1929 81872
The sign on the creeper-clad walls of the Old Bridge Hotel proclaim it as 'one of England's best'. That was in 1929: even today, this elegant 18th century hotel enjoys a reputation for the opulence of its decoration.

BRAMPTON, CHURCH STREET c1955 B182020
The famous diarist Samuel Pepys often came to Brampton, visiting his uncle. Pepys himself always wanted to retire to this pretty village, although he ended his days in Clapham. His sister, Mrs Paulina Jackson, was the last member of the family to live here, and a monument to her can be seen in St Mary's church.

BRAMPTON, HIGH STREET c1955 B182015
Back in the 1950s it would have been quite normal for a bank to have a branch in a small village. Rationalisation has seen a good many of them close down.

BUCKDEN, CHURCH STREET 1906 55429
The man with the horse and cart on the left is at the village pump, which is situated in front of the Methodist Chapel.

BUCKDEN, THE CHURCH 1906 55431
Although the church of St Mary's has many interesting points, clearly the main object of interest in this picture is the building next door, Buckden Palace. Although but a fraction of the original 15th century palace, this nevertheless impressive building was the residence of the Bishops of Lincoln up until 1842. Katherine of Aragon was imprisoned in one of the corner turrets for a year after her marriage to Henry VIII was annulled.

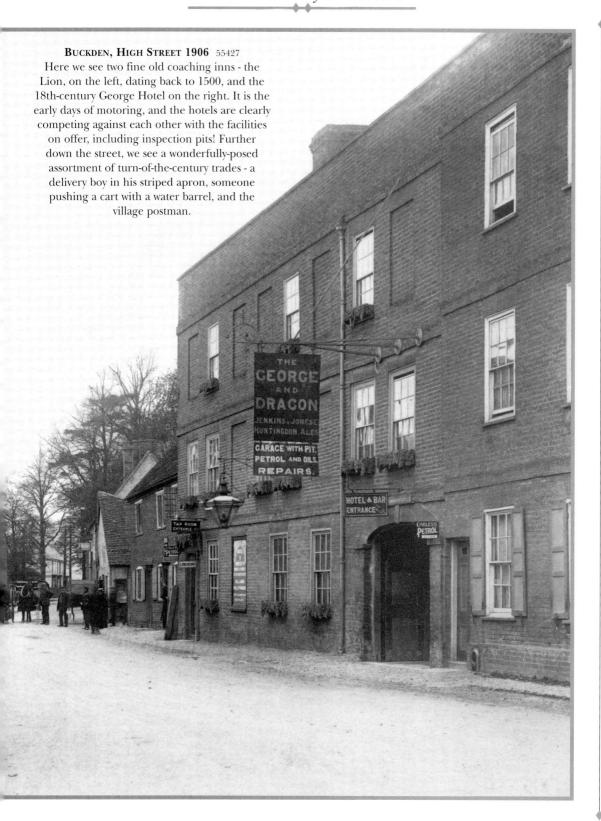

BUCKDEN, HIGH STREET 1906 55427
Here we see two fine old coaching inns - the
Lion, on the left, dating back to 1500, and the
18th-century George Hotel on the right. It is the
early days of motoring, and the hotels are clearly
competing against each other with the facilities
on offer, including inspection pits! Further
down the street, we see a wonderfully-posed
assortment of turn-of-the-century trades - a
delivery boy in his striped apron, someone
pushing a cart with a water barrel, and the
village postman.

BUCKDEN, THE VILLAGE c1950 B237010
It is just over forty years after photograph No 55427, and doubtless the inspection pits are not quite the selling point they once were! And whilst the general level of signs outside has reduced, AA and RAC signs are prominent on both buildings.

ST NEOTS, HIGH STREET 1897 39975
This Victorian street scene combines bystanders quite obviously enthralled with the activities of the photographer, who are standing still enough to be captured in sharp detail, with people going about their business, whose movement registers as blurs; the person crossing to the pavement on the left-hand side almost appears to have only one leg!

ST NEOTS, THE PAPER MILLS 1897 39988

Vast quantities of water are required to manufacture paper, hence the situation of the paper mill at St Neots on the Great Ouse. But whilst a lot of Victorian industrial architecture has a certain charm, there is certainly none apparent here.

ST NEOTS, AERIAL VIEW C1955 S37013

A priory was founded here in the 10th century in honour of the Cornish St Neot, which was later replaced by a Benedictine monastery. The town originally stood on higher agricultural land, and its position on the Ouse was not exploited until the middle ages, with the growth of a market.

St Neots, High Street 1925 77204
There is an interesting mix of trades in one building on the far side of the road: a hairdresser and piano shop.
What would that inspire - 'Chop-sticks', perhaps? Or maybe 'Hair on a G String'...

EATON SOCON, THE MILL AND THE GREAT OUSE c1960 E202019
This part of the Great Ouse has several mills at Eaton Socon, and also at St Neots. But the scene to the left of the picture rather bears out the fact that modern industrialisation has rather left the waterways to the leisure boaters.

GAMLINGAY, MILL STREET c1965 G277007
Situated on the Cambridgeshire border with Bedfordshire, Gamlingay was once a thriving market town. After a disastrous fire in 1600 which nearly destroyed the entire town, the market was moved to nearby Potton, in Bedfordshire.

GREAT STAUGHTON, THE VILLAGE c1955 G279009
Great Staughton grew up as a roadside settlement along the road between St Neots and Kimbolton. St Andrew's church appears to have spent most of its existence going through periods of boom or decline, with major reconstructions taking place in the 15th, 17th and 19th centuries.

KIMBOLTON, HIGH STREET c1955 K157021
Mainly Georgian houses front Kimbolton's wide High Street, laid out in medieval times to accommodate a market. At the end of the street is Kimbolton Castle, first built around 1200, later a Tudor house and the place where Katherine of Aragon died in 1536. The castle was remodelled in the early 18th century by Vanbrugh, with a screen by Robert Adam.

KIMBOLTON, HIGH STREET c1955 K157001

This view looks away from Kimbolton Castle along the High Street. Although most of the frontages are Georgian, with a pleasing variation in roof lines, many of the houses are actually a good deal older. The 13th century church spire, with its three tiers of lucarnes - the windows which pierce it - appears above the rooftops.

ELLINGTON, THE VILLAGE 1906 55436

With just a sprinkling of snow, this delightful scene could very easily make a traditional Christmas card! Ellington's church is mentioned in the Domesday Survey of 1086, but the oldest surviving part of the building dates back to the 13th century. The spire was restored in 1899, and the nave roof about a year after this photograph.

SPALDWICK, THE VILLAGE 1906 55433

The village of Spaldwick lies at the centre of a medieval estate which included most of the neighbouring settlements. The church in the background is known as 'the cathedral of the valley'.

OLD WESTON, THE POST OFFICE c1955 O113007

Old Weston is fragmented as a village, with the church standing somewhat detached from the main part of it. The village originally extended beyond the church, but was lost in a devastating fire in 1701.

STILTON, CHURCH STREET C1955 S673012

Stilton is a small village south of Peterborough, with a reputation from ages past for a cheese which it has never actually produced. The village was an important staging point on the Great North Road. Leicestershire farmers took their produce to the 17th century Bell Inn for delivery by coach to London, where the cheese became known as Stilton.

STILTON, FEN STREET C1955 S673004

These brick-built cottages simply ooze charm, even if some of them appear to be in need of attention. Note the cross-shaped ends to the tie-bars which help prevent the walls from bowing out on the house next to the telegraph pole, and on the next but one along.

CASTOR, PETERBOROUGH ROAD c1955 C584016
Castor stands on the junction of the two main Roman roads in this part of Cambridgeshire, Ermine Street and King's Street. Excavations here during the 19th century uncovered a wealth of Roman buildings and pottery.

CASTOR, THE VILLAGE c1955 C584003
This view looks west along the main road through Castor towards Ailsworth. Both villages feature many delightful stone and timber houses.

Index

Frith Book Co Titles

Frith Book Company publish over a 100 new titles each year. For latest catalogue please contact Frith Book Co.

Town Books 96pp, 100 photos. County and Themed Books 128pp, 150 photos
(unless specified) All titles hardback laminated case and jacket
except those indicated pb (paperback)

Around Barnstaple	1-85937-084-5	£12.99
Around Blackpool	1-85937-049-7	£12.99
Around Bognor Regis	1-85937-055-1	£12.99
Around Bristol	1-85937-050-0	£12.99
Around Cambridge	1-85937-092-6	£12.99
Cheshire	1-85937-045-4	£14.99
Around Chester	1-85937-090-X	£12.99
Around Chesterfield	1-85937-071-3	£12.99

Around Maidstone	1-85937-056-X	£12.99
North Yorkshire	1-85937-048-9	£14.99
Around Nottingham	1-85937-060-8	£12.99
Around Penzance	1-85937-069-1	£12.99
Around Reading	1-85937-087-X	£12.99
Around St Ives	1-85937-068-3	£12.99
Around Salisbury	1-85937-091-8	£12.99
Around Scarborough	1-85937-104-3	£12.99
Scottish Castles	1-85937-077-2	£14.99
Around Sevenoaks and Tonbridge	1-85937-057-8	£12.99
Sheffield and S Yorkshire	1-85937-070-5	£14.99
Shropshire	1-85937-083-7	£14.99
Staffordshire	1-85937-047-0 (96pp)	£12.99
Suffolk	1-85937-074-8	£14.99
Surrey	1-85937-081-0	£14.99
Torbay	1-85937-063-2	£12.99
Wiltshire	1-85937-053-5	£14.99

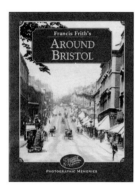

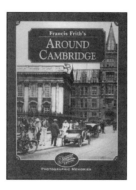

Around Chichester	1-85937-089-6	£12.99
Cornwall	1-85937-054-3	£14.99
Cotswolds	1-85937-099-3	£14.99
Around Derby	1-85937-046-2	£12.99
Devon	1-85937-052-7	£14.99
Dorset	1-85937-075-6	£14.99
Dorset Coast	1-85937-062-4	£14.99
Around Dublin	1-85937-058-6	£12.99
East Anglia	1-85937-059-4	£14.99
Around Eastbourne	1-85937-061-6	£12.99
English Castles	1-85937-078-0	£14.99
Around Falmouth	1-85937-066-7	£12.99
Hampshire	1-85937-064-0	£14.99
Isle of Man	1-85937-065-9	£14.99

British Life A Century Ago

246 x 189mm 144pp, hardback. Black and white Lavishly illustrated with photos from the turn of the century, and with extensive commentary. It offers a unique insight into the social history and heritage of bygone Britain.

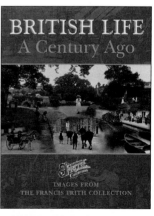

1-85937-103-5 £17.99

Available from your local bookshop or from the publisher

Frith Book Co Titles Available in 2000

Around Bakewell	1-85937-1132	£12.99	Feb
Around Bath	1-85937-097-7	£12.99	Feb
Around Belfast	1-85937-094-2	£12.99	Feb
Around Bournemouth	1-85937-067-5	£12.99	Feb
Cambridgeshire	1-85937-086-1	£14.99	Feb
Essex	1-85937-082-9	£14.99	Feb
Greater Manchester	1-85937-108-6	£14.99	Feb
Around Guildford	1-85937-117-5	£12.99	Feb
Around Harrogate	1-85937-112-4	£12.99	Feb
Hertfordshire	1-85937-079-9	£14.99	Feb
Isle of Wight	1-85937-114-0	£14.99	Feb
Around Lincoln	1-85937-111-6	£12.99	Feb
Margate/Ramsgate	1-85937-116-7	£12.99	Feb
Northumberland and Tyne & Wear			
	1-85937-072-1	£14.99	Feb
Around Newark	1-85937-105-1	£12.99	Feb
Around Oxford	1-85937-096-9	£12.99	Feb
Oxfordshire	1-85937-076-4	£14.99	Feb
Around Shrewsbury	1-85937-110-8	£12.99	Feb
South Devon Coast	1-85937-107-8	£14.99	Feb
Around Southport	1-85937-106-x	£12.99	Feb
West Midlands	1-85937-109-4	£14.99	Feb
Cambridgeshire	1-85937-086-1	£14.99	Mar
County Durham	1-85937-123-x	£14.99	Mar
Cumbria	1-85937-101-9	£14.99	Mar
Down the Severn	1-85937-118-3	£14.99	Mar
Down the Thames	1-85937-121-3	£14.99	Mar
Around Exeter	1-85937-126-4	£12.99	Mar
Around Folkestone	1-85937-124-8	£12.99	Mar
Gloucestershire	1-85937-102-7	£14.99	Mar
Around Great Yarmouth			
	1-85937-085-3	£12.99	Mar
Kent Living Memories	1-85937-125-6	£14.99	Mar
Around Leicester	1-85937-073-x	£12.99	Mar
Around Liverpool	1-85937-051-9	£12.99	Mar
Around Plymouth	1-85937-119-1	£12.99	Mar
Around Portsmouth	1-85937-122-1	£12.99	Mar
Around Southampton	1-85937-088-8	£12.99	Mar
Around Stratford upon Avon			
	1-85937-098-5	£12.99	Mar
Welsh Castles	1-85937-120-5	£14.99	Mar
Canals and Waterways	1-85937-129-9	£17.99	Apr
East Sussex	1-85937-130-2	£14.99	Apr
Exmoor	1-85937-132-9	£14.99	Apr
Farms and Farming	1-85937-134-5	£17.99	Apr
Around Horsham	1-85937-127-2	£12.99	Apr
Ipswich (pb)	1-85937-133-7	£12.99	Apr
Ireland (pb)	1-85937-181-7	£9.99	Apr
London (pb)	1-85937-183-3	£9.99	Apr
New Forest	1-85937-128-0	£14.99	Apr
Scotland	1-85937-182-5	£9.99	Apr
Stone Circles & Ancient Monuments			
	1-85937-143-4	£17.99	Apr
Sussex (pb)	1-85937-184-1	£9.99	Apr
Colchester (pb)	1-85937-188-4	£8.99	May
County Maps of Britain			
	1-85937-156-6 (192pp)	£19.99	May
Around Harrow	1-85937-141-8	£12.99	May
Leicestershire (pb)	1-85937-185-x	£9.99	May
Lincolnshire	1-85937-135-3	£14.99	May
Around Newquay	1-85937-140-x	£12.99	May
Nottinghamshire (pb)	1-85937-187-6	£9.99	May
Redhill to Reigate	1-85937-137-x	£12.99	May
Scilly Isles	1-85937-136-1	£14.99	May
Victorian & Edwardian Yorkshire			
	1-85937-154-x	£14.99	May
Around Winchester	1-85937-139-6	£12.99	May
Yorkshire (pb)	1-85937-186-8	£9.99	May
Berkshire (pb)	1-85937-191-4	£9.99	Jun
Brighton (pb)	1-85937-192-2	£8.99	Jun
Dartmoor	1-85937-145-0	£14.99	Jun
East London	1-85937-080-2	£14.99	Jun
Glasgow (pb)	1-85937-190-6	£8.99	Jun
Kent (pb)	1-85937-189-2	£9.99	Jun
Victorian & Edwardian Kent			
	1-85937-149-3	£14.99	Jun
North Devon Coast	1-85937-146-9	£14.99	Jun
Peak District	1-85937-100-0	£14.99	Jun
Around Truro	1-85937-147-7	£12.99	Jun
Victorian & Edwardian Maritime Album			
	1-85937-144-2	£14.99	Jun
West Sussex	1-85937-148-5	£14.99	Jun

FRITH PRODUCTS & SERVICES

Francis Frith would doubtless be pleased to know that the pioneering publishing venture he started in 1860 still continues today. More than a hundred and thirty years later, The Francis Frith Collection continues in the same innovative tradition and is now one of the foremost publishers of vintage photographs in the world. Some of the current activities include:

Interior Decoration

Today Frith's photographs can be seen framed and as giant wall murals in thousands of pubs, restaurants, hotels, banks, retail stores and other public buildings throughout the country. In every case they enhance the unique local atmosphere of the places they depict and provide reminders of gentler days in an increasingly busy and frenetic world.

Product Promotions

Frith products have been used by many major companies to promote the sales of their own products or to reinforce their own history and heritage. Brands include Hovis bread, Courage beers, Scots Porage Oats, Colman's mustard, Cadbury's foods, Mellow Birds coffee, Dunhill pipe tobacco, Guinness, and Bulmer's Cider.

Genealogy and Family History

As the interest in family history and roots grows world-wide, more and more people are turning to Frith's photographs of Great Britain for images of the towns, villages and streets where their ancestors lived; and, of course, photographs of the churches and chapels where their ancestors were christened, married and buried are an essential part of every genealogy tree and family album.

A series of easy-to-use CD Roms is planned for publication, and an increasing number of Frith photographs will be able to be viewed on specialist genealogy sites. A growing range of Frith books will be available on CD.

The Internet

Already thousands of Frith photographs can be viewed and purchased on the internet. By the end of the year 2000 some 60,000 Frith photographs will be available on the internet. The number of sites is constantly expanding, each focussing on different products and services from the Collection.

Some of the sites are listed below.

www.townpages.co.uk
www.icollector.com
www.barclaysquare.co.uk
www.cornwall-online.co.uk

For background information on the Collection look at the two following sites:

www.francisfrith.com
www.francisfrith.co.uk
www.frithbook.co.uk

Frith Products

All Frith photographs are available Framed or just as Mounted Prints, and can be ordered from the address below. From time to time other products - Address Books, Calendars, Table Mats, Postcards etc - are available.

The Frith Collectors' Guild

In response to the many customers who enjoy collecting Frith photographs we have created the Frith Collectors' Guild. Members are entitled to a range of benefits, including a regular magazine, special discounts and special limited edition products.

For further information: if you would like further information on any of the above aspects of the Frith business please contact us at the address below:

The Francis Frith Collection, Frith's Barn, Teffont, Salisbury, Wiltshire England SP3 5QP.

Tel: +44 (0) 1722 716 376 Fax: +44 (0) 1722 716 881 Email: uksales@francisfrith.com

To receive your FREE Mounted Print

Cut out this Voucher and return it with your remittance for £1.50 to cover postage and handling. Choose any photograph included in this book. Your SEPIA print will be A4 in size, and mounted in a cream mount with burgundy rule lines, overall size 14 x 11 inches.

Order additional Mounted Prints at HALF PRICE (only £7.49 each*)

If there are further pictures you would like to order, possibly as gifts for friends and family, acquire them at half price (no additional postage and handling required).

Have your Mounted Prints framed*

For an additional £14.95 per print you can have your chosen Mounted Print framed in an elegant polished wood and gilt moulding, overall size 16 x 13 inches (no additional postage and handling required).

---

* IMPORTANT!
These special prices are only available if ordered using the original voucher on this page (no copies permitted) and at the same time as your free Mounted Print, for delivery to the same address

---

Voucher for FREE and Reduced Price Frith Prints

Picture no.	Page number	Qty	Mounted @ £7.49	Framed + £14.95	Total Cost
		1	**Free of charge***	£	£
			£	£	£
			£	£	£
			£	£	£
			£	£	£
			£	£	£
			* Post & handling		£1.50

Book Title . . . .   **Total Order Cost** | £

Please do not photocopy this voucher. Only the original is valid, so please cut it out and return it to us.

I enclose a cheque / postal order for £ . . . .
made payable to 'The Francis Frith Collection'
OR please debit my Mastercard / Visa / Switch / Amex card

Number . . . .

Expires . . . .   Signature . . . .

Name Mr/Mrs/Ms . . . .

Address . . . .

. . . .

. . . .

. . . . Postcode . . . .

Daytime Tel No . . . .   Valid to 31/12/01

Frith Collectors' Guild

From time to time we publish a magazine of news and stories about Frith photographs and further special offers of Frith products. If you would like 12 months FREE membership, please return this form.

Send completed forms to:
**The Francis Frith Collection,
Frith's Barn, Teffont, Salisbury,
Wiltshire SP3 5QP**

The Francis Frith Collectors' Guild

Please enrol me as a member for 12 months free of charge.

Name Mr/Mrs/Ms . . . .

Address . . . .

. . . .

. . . .

. . . . Postcode . . . .

Free Print - see overleaf